101 BEST FOOD RULES

Accelerate Your Progress Towards Permanent Weight Loss by Leveraging the Most Effective Rules Created by Hundreds of Successful Never Binge Again Readers (and Clients!)

Glenn Livingston Ph.D.

INTRODUCTION

Why I Wrote *This* Book

It's been 3½ years since I published Never Binge Again, the "stop overeating now" book with 700,000+ readers and 2,000+ reviews...free for Kindle, Nook, and/or PDF at www.NeverBingeAgain.com. During this time, I've had hundreds of clients, and supervised several other coaches to help with client demand. Collectively we've done thousands of sessions and seen the first-hand results of virtually every Food Rule you could imagine.

From this experience, we've learned which rules are more effective, and which engender struggle. This book outlines the best rules from successful Never Binge Again implementers in real life, along with an interpretation in many cases of WHY the rules work so well. It's intended as a companion to Never Binge Again which can help strengthen and speed your journey into a more peaceful relationship with food.

Moreover, I've chosen this book to present several important subtleties about Food Plans, Food Rules, and Guidelines which were too detailed and analytical for the main book...but which the more interested reader can benefit from immensely. Things like why Never Rules work better than Always Rules, the discovery of a new rule category, how to choose between Never vs. Conditional Rules, etc.

The insights and rules you'll read in here were all gleaned from real people struggling with real food issues in the real world.

One last thing, and it's important: The idea in this book is AB-SOLUTELY NOT to provide a comprehensive list of Food Rules we want everyone to follow. That would almost certainly overwhelm you and throw you off track! The goal is to provide examples of successful rules, so you can learn from the best of the best, and decide for yourself which you may wish to incorporate. You'll see the way successful Never Binge Againers implement the method, with the benefit of my professional rationale for why it works.

Why Listen to Me?

If you don't know already, I'm a psychologist and formerly fat guy who suffered from compulsive overeating for approximately 30 years before tripping on an odd method to solve the problem. I'm also the former CEO of two companies which sold more than $30,000,000 in marketing consulting to Fortune 500 companies, many in the Big Food industry. *(I regret that last part now)*. You might have seen my and/or my previous companies' work in The New York Times, Crain's NY Business, ABC and/or CBS radio, Bloomberg Radio, and dozens of other major media outlets. I've also built and sold a digital advertising agency, built a coach training business which competed on the world stage, and published Never Binge Again which, at the time of this publication, had hovered at and/or near the #1 position on Amazon for almost three years in the weight loss category for kindle. If you'd like to know more about me, read the detailed introduction please in Never Binge Again and/or 45 Binge Trigger Busters.

OK – enough said. Now that you know why I wrote this book and who I am, let's start with some of the most powerful insights about the rules in general. Then we'll get to specific, effective Food Rule examples.

CHAPTER 1: SIX INSIGHTS TO MAKE YOUR FOOD PLAN MORE POWERFUL

There are six essential insights we've gleaned from coaching clients over the years which can make *your* Food Plan dramatically more powerful, easier to comply with, and simpler to resume if you make a mistake. In order they are (1) Translating "Always" rules to "Never" rules whenever possible; (2) A NEW rule category; (3) Skillfully reducing the number of Food Rules on your Food Plan; (4) Separating Guidelines from Food Rules; (5) Separating Definitions from Food Rules; (6) Always using the full articulation of the Food Rules, not shortcuts.

Let's go through each one in detail.

Insight #1 – Never Rules Work Better Than Always Rules

About two years into coaching Never Binge Again clients I started noticing something very interesting: People had a harder time implementing the "Always" rules as compared to Nevers, and they were more successful if I could help them translate their Always rules into a Never and/or a Conditional.

For the purposes of our discussion here, please note Conditionals Rules are really just special cases of Never Rules. The distinguishing feature between Never vs. Conditional is that the Never category is reserved for foods, substances, and behaviors the user wishes to give up entirely. The conditional category is for those where the user wishes to allow more leeway.

Despite this difference, both the Conditional and Never categories require people to attend to something they must NOT do. For example, "I will never eat chocolate on a weekday again" *(a Conditional Food Rule)* still utilizes the terms "Never" and "Again" to lock down something the user will NEVER do, just like "I will never eat chocolate again" *(a Never Food Rule).*

This is important because for BOTH Nevers and Conditionals the cognitive processing goes something like this:

> ➤ **Trigger Food and/or Situation → I want to do something → But I never do → OK, I won't do it.** *(My Pig wants it, not me!)*

Never and Conditional Rules BOTH rely on this logic. There is some strong desire which arises in the brain, usually in response to an external stimulus, and then this desire is then negated by the rule. The desire is already there, as is the link to the previously unwanted behavior.

This is NOT the case for Always rules.

When you attempt to implement a rule like "I always drink a half gallon of pure spring water every day", there is NO desire to drink a half gallon water present to begin with. A need, perhaps, but a desire, no. Furthermore, there is NO pre-existing LINK to a natural desire and/or behavior, so the user needs to find a way to PUT IT on their mind when it doesn't naturally enter. Otherwise, there's nothing for the cognitive rule to act on:

> ➤ **Blank Mind Regarding Behavior → No Interest In Doing Anything in Particular → Nothing For The Rule To Act Upon**

See the problem?

Now, some people DO implement always rules effectively, usually by installing reminders in convenient places. For example, I know a guy who reliably implemented the rule "I always write out a hypothetical food plan for the next day" by putting a note on his pillow that said "Write your food plan." I also know a woman who "always eats one piece of fruit three times per day" by not allowing herself to begin any meal without one.

These successful Always Rule implementers translated their Always Rules into Never Rules without knowing it! This linked their rules to a naturally occurring thought or desire in the brain and gave their Always Rule something to act upon... the key to achieving their goal.

For example, the gentleman above was unknowingly translating "I always write out my food plan for the next day" to *"I will **Never** lay down in bed for the night again without first writing my hypothetical food plan for the next day."* In this way, he linked the desired behavior (writing his food plan) to a pre-existing desire and behavioral routine... lying down for bed. He knew he was destined to WANT to lay down every night. THAT impulse was already too well ingrained in his behavioral routine to skip. Therefore, he could 100% count on the desire that would reliably trigger his brain to act on the rule.

Similarly, the fruit-eating woman knew she was going to have at least three meals per day no matter what. She unconsciously translated her rule to "I will never again begin a meal without eating one piece of fruit."

The solution is to find a naturally occurring, reliable desire and translate your Always into a Never which requires you to execute the target behavior before gratifying that desire! It's best to find a desire which occurs naturally during the time of day when you want to perform the activity. For example, if you want to perform the activity in the morning, perhaps you can link it to your morning coffee. If it's at night, then you might link your Always to something you must do before you sit down for the evening to watch TV with the spouse, etc.

Here's one more example:

> ➤ ALWAYS: "I always spend at least 10 minutes per Calendar Day on my treadmill, unless I have a fever and/or am sleeping outside the home."

> ➤ NEVER: "I will never again go to bed without having spent 10 minutes on my treadmill unless I have a fever and/or am sleeping outside the home."

See how this works?

There's one more subtle reason Never Rules work better than Always Rules. This has to do with the word "Again." See, combining the words Never and Again in a rule makes an extremely powerful statement to your Pig, and stops it from persistently suggesting "That rule doesn't still apply, does it?"

Never Again means from now until the end of the universe, and all future universes… until the end of time itself. Eternity is a very, very long time, and your Pig knows that.

The problem with Always rules is that the word "Again" doesn't pair well with it linguistically, so your Pig can say "Oh, are we still doing that? I thought we stopped that one a while ago. Enough already!"

See what I mean?

Never Rules work substantially better than Always Rules because they link to existing desires and can be more easily locked down FOREVER with language. If you're having trouble sticking to your Always Rules, translate them to Nevers as per above. Another reason why connecting a rule to an existing desire works so well is that when you gratify the desire after the link is established, the gratification acts as a reward. So you train yourself that you get a reward for completing the action. It's Pavlovian and silly. But it works. *(For example, you WANT to go to bed when you're tired in the evening, but you can't do it until you walk on the treadmill. So going to bed becomes a reward for using the treadmill. See what I mean?)*

Insight #2 - "Only" – Another Powerful Rules Category

The more simply you state your rule, the easier it will be to remember, and the less brain-glucose *(willpower)* you'll have to burn to implement it when the situation arises.

I first discovered this when I was attempting to make a complex set of conditional rules to govern my eating during a stressful business trip. I'd been feeling extraordinarily tempted to listen to my Pig about all sorts of things when I was overtired, overstressed, and wandering around in airport after airport. I remember feeling particularly tempted to have vegan sushi *(I can't eat cooked grains for medical reasons)*, sautéed vegetables from the Asian place *(entirely too salty for my medical needs)*, and baked potatoes *(also off limits for medical reasons)*. I was also tempted by the food served on the airplane itself – which was generally disgusting and unhealthy by my standards.

After agonizing over countless variations of conditional travel rules, something extremely simple occurred to me... what if I ONLY ate fruit and vegetables? I knew nothing would happen to me from previous nutritional research. Besides, it was only a couple of days. "I will only ever eat fruit and vegetables at airports and on airplanes."

That did the trick. No matter what I encountered in the airport I just echoed in my head "I only eat fruit and vegetables." I didn't even have to add the conditional part in my head at that time because I was already in the airport and I knew it. "I only eat fruit and vegetables" was ridiculously simple, and it worked.

The "Only" category works very well when there are too many Nevers to list out and remember. For example, when I'm helping people figure out how to get off sugar, I'll often ask them to define it inclusively vs. exclusively. What are the ONLY sweet tastes you'll ever eat again?

> ➤ "The *only* sweet tastes I'll ever eat again are whole fruit and berries."

> ➤ "The *only* sweet tastes I'll ever eat again are whole fruit, berries, sugar free gum, stevia, and honey."

See how it works?

The technical form of the Only Rules is "I will only ever do_____ again when _____" or "The only _____ I will ever eat and/or drink again are _____"

And there's often a linguistic shortcut you can use at the moment of temptation "I only eat _____."

Linguistically, the word Ever in an Only Rule serves the same function as Never.

Insight #3 - Fewer Rules are Better – Especially in the Beginning

The most important thing you can do in the beginning is set yourself up for success. ANY success.

See, most people who've been struggling with overeating have been doing so for decades and their Pigs have them beat down so hard about it they can barely catch their breath between episodes. It says things like "You've tried some many times and failed, why will this time be any different?" "You're pathetic, just give up and become a happy fat person – when will you finally just accept your fate!?"… and we unfortunately believe them.

In the long run, people start to feel as if they are truly powerless over food. As if some unexplainable force could take over inside them and force them to use their arms, legs, mouth, and tongue to eat unimaginable and undesirable amount of Pig Slop. I've actually had people tell me that they "go unconscious" during a Binge. *(You don't, as evidenced by the fact you'll be able to remember where you got and ate the first bite, what the checkout person looked like at the supermarket, how you got to the store, etc.)*

So first and foremost, we must overcome this perception. We simply must prove to your Pig that You are in control, in even the smallest way. This is why I often ask people *"What is the smallest, simplest rule you can make which you know you CAN AND WILL do, but which will also make a significant difference and start things moving in the right direction again?"*

It could be anything from "I'll never go back for seconds again" to "I'll never eat in front of the TV again" to "I will never eat breakfast without first weighing myself again", etc.

Something. ANYTHING. Make it simple.

Then, after you've proven to your Pig that you know what you're doing and You are in control, you can ratchet things up a bit to start working on weight loss, etc.

If you're struggling, simplify.

This applies to your Food Plan as a whole once you've got more than one Food Rule too. Less rules are better, but make sure all the "dangerous intersections" (your trigger foods and behaviors) are covered.

I once had a mentor who I asked how long my persuasive copywriting sales-letters should be. He said "Glenn, it's like a woman's dress. It's got to be long enough to cover the good parts, but short enough to keep it interesting." Of course, that didn't give me any hard and fast limits, but I got the point. I'd write all my persuasive points, then edit out the garbage and redundancy.

I think the same thing can be said about Food Plans as a whole. Make sure you cover all the important parts but get rid of any redundant and/or unnecessary rules. Also, if it feels like you've got too many rules the odds are good you're trying to manage something conditionally which might be better off in the Never category. It's up to you, but I've seen this 4,637+ times.

Insight #4 - Separate Guidelines from Rules

A lot of clients seem to confuse guidelines vs. Never Binge Again Food Rules. A Food Rule is something extremely objective and externally verifiable. 10 observers could follow you around for a month and agree 100% whether you did or didn't follow it. A Guideline, on the other hand, is a nice principle to be reminded of, but one which can't be 100% verified and agreed upon by neutral observers.

This is an important distinction because the Pig thrives on ambiguous rules, and a Guideline, by its nature, always contains at least some ambiguity. For example, "I'll only eat when I'm hungry and always stop when I'm full" is a nice guiding principle. A good North Star to aim for. There's nothing wrong with wanting to remind yourself of this every day and do your very best to achieve it...

But it's still too ambiguous to be an NBA Food Rule. Neutral observes wouldn't know if you were truly hungry 100% of the time you ate, and whether you stopped 100% of the time when you were full. As a result, you won't be able to 100% discern your own thoughts from the Pig's thoughts about it. "Oh baby, you're definitely hungry" – Sincerely, Your Pig. Or "Nah, we're not too full yet, just a few more bites" – Sincerely, Your Pig.

See the problem?

But we don't want to throw out the baby with the bathwater. Guidelines can be very helpful goal posts to keep in mind, even though we can never know if we've 100% achieved them. I therefore recommend keeping a separate Guidelines section of your Food Plan. I usually put them underneath the main matrix to distinguish them from Food Rules. It's critically important to avoid mixing them up because that can lead to blurring the lines on your ACTUAL Food Rules, which allows ambiguity to creep in, and the Pig to blast through.

Some additional example Guidelines might be "I always buy organic food whenever remotely possible" *(that's one from my personal Food Plan)*, or "I always try to be in bed by 10 pm" *(useful to allow for occasional but not strictly defined exceptions).*

Separate your Guidelines from your Food Rules. Make sure your Rules are all 100% verifiable by external observation. You'll thank me for this, I promise!

Insight #5 - Separate Definitions from Rules

It's important to keep your Food Rules as simple as possible, both so you'll remember them, but also so they require a minimum of cognitive effort to execute. In short, because there is such a strong impulse to allow the reptilian brain to take over during moments of temptation *(perceived feast or famine—or fight or flight—revs up the body's emergency defenses)*, and because thinking is MUCH more of a higher brain function, you want to keep the need to THINK to a minimum. Your Food Rules should be as short as you can make them, as simple as you can make them, and as powerful as you can make them.

For this reason, it's helpful to move any definitions to a separate section of your Food Plan. For example, consider the following list of Conditional Rules:

FOOD PLAN RULES COMBINED WITH DEFINITIONS

➤   I will never eat Sugar again. Sugar is anything sweet besides whole fruit, berries, stevia, sugar-free gum, up to one teaspoon of honey in my coffee and/or tea, and any processed and labeled food with ANY sweetener listed above the 5th ingredient on the label.

➤   I will never eat pasta again other than at a Work Function and/ or on a Major Holiday, but never more than twice per Calendar Week in any case. A Work Function is anything I am required to attend by my superiors where food and/or alcohol is served. Major Holidays include Thanksgiving, Christmas, New Year's Day, Easter, and Memorial Day.

➤ I will only ever eat dessert at a Restaurant Function again. A Restaurant Function is any meal served outside my home which has been prepared by someone else, and which I eat with at least one other person sitting at my table.

The definitions themselves are sound, but they are presented in a way which is a little cumbersome and difficult to remember. It would be better to separate them as follows:

FOOD PLAN RULES SEPARATED FROM DEFINITIONS

Food Rules

➤ I will never eat Sugar again.

➤ I will never eat pasta again except for Work Functions and/or on a Major Holidays, but no more than twice per Calendar Week.

➤ I will only ever eat dessert again at a Restaurant Function, but no more than twice per Calendar Week.

Definitions

➤ SUGAR: Sugar is anything sweet besides whole fruit, berries, stevia, sugar-free gum, up to one teaspoon of honey in my coffee and/or tea, and any processed and labeled food with ANY sweetener listed above the 5th ingredient on the label.

➤ WORK FUNCTION: A Work Function is anything I am required to attend by my superiors where food and/or alcohol is served.

➤ MAJOR HOLIDAY: Major Holidays are limited to Thanksgiving, Christmas, New Year's Day, Easter, and Memorial Day.

➤ RESTAURANT FUNCTION: A Restaurant Function is any meal served outside my home which has been prepared by someone else, and which I eat with at least one other person sitting at my table.

➤ CALENDAR WEEK: A Calendar Week begins on Sunday and ends on Saturday.

See how much simpler and clearer that is? This allows you to concentrate on the Food Rules, which you should read every day for the first 90 days. Consult the definitions section only when you feel unclear and/or need to remember the "acid test." *(NOTE: The astute reader will also observe I found a few places to tighten up the language even further while separating the rules from the definitions.)*

Insight #6 – Use the Full Articulation of the Food Rule

Clients are prone to letting their Pigs convince them to use short-cuts for their Rules. For example, rather than articulating the full Food Rule "I will never eat chocolate again" on their Food Plan, they write "No chocolate." "It's so much simpler this way", their Pigs say, fully aware that this shortcut is much, MUCH easier to assail.

See, when you tell your Pig "never again" you cut off ALL possibilities. Never again means forever, as in forever and ever and ever, until the universe is entirely dark, NOTHING left to eat, and NO food decisions to make. Never again implies eternity. This is a life sentence for your Pig and it knows it. Prisoners given a life sentence eventually give up hope. They don't WANT hope, because hope in a hopeless situation is painful. Like being constantly sexually stimulated in a situation where there is no possibility of release. Who wants that frustration?

But when you say "no chocolate" your Pig assumes you mean "no chocolate today but maybe tomorrow." You're giving your Pig a realistic chance. You're giving it HOPE. And when the Pig has even a shred of hope it will go to the ends of the earth to convince you. It will pull out all the stops. It will beg and plead and cajole you. It will come up with the most persuasive, most interesting arguments you've ever heard. Things you've never thought of... things you could never imagine. Give the Pig even one ounce of hope and it will ruthlessly and consistently Squeal at you until you give in. But give it a life sentence and it settles down to accept its fate.

Include the words "Never" and "Again" whenever you can in your Food Rules. Combined with insight #1 (nevers work better than always) this is a powerful one-two knockout punch. And remember, you can and should use the words "never again" in Conditional Rules too. For example: "I will never again eat chocolate on a weekday."

Of course, You can change your Food Plan whenever you want to, as long as you do it with forethought and consideration *(read Never Binge Again for free if you don't understand this)*, but we need to present it to the Pig as if it were set in stone. Like telling a two-year-old child she can never ever cross the street without holding your hand, even though you know when she's older you'll teach her how. You "lie" to her and present the rule as if it were set in stone because she's not mature enough to even consider darting across the street by herself. Our Pigs act like a two-year-old with Pig Slop. Plus, it's OK to lie to your Pig, it's been lying to you for decades and causing you to slowly self-destruct.

OK, those are the new Food Plan and Food Rule insights. They're worth reading twice and carefully integrating into your own Food Plan. They really do help with compliance, and even more so with clarity of mind.

Now, on to the Food Rules.

Oh, there's one more thing and it's VERY IMPORTANT...

You do NOT need to implement all these rules! It's more like a menu at a restaurant, you choose one or two things which might be helpful, you don't order every dish on the page *(despite what your Pig might want you to do).*

CHAPTER 2: NEVERS

Food

As you might expect, our successful clients often had a Never Rule in place. Nevers are very powerful, but there's nothing particularly interesting or unusual about the way people articulate the rule, so there's not much to explain and/or focus on. The things many of our clients had eliminated from their lives completely with good results included but were not limited to donuts, sugar, flour, wheat, gluten, candy, cookies, cake, ice cream, fast food, French fries, chips *(or "crisps" in the U.K.)*, soda, butter, dairy, nuts, salty snacks, chocolate, animal foods, and more.

There are just a few useful observations regarding implementation of Never Rules:

➢ SUGAR: The most important concerns Sugar. When people chose to never eat sugar again, it was important to be very specific about how they defined sugar itself. Rather than "I will never eat sugar again" I usually suggest people phrase their rule: "I will never eat anything sweet again besides X, Y, Z, etc." Defining it this way *(inclusively vs. exclusively)* prevents the Pig from coming up with endless forms of hidden sugar which are "not really sugar", etc. (Note: In the U.K., nutrition labeling allows for rules such as "I will never eat any processed food with more than 3% sugar on the label again" but this rule is difficult to implement elsewhere.)

➢ FLOUR: The same type of reasoning goes for flour, if you're going to allow any at all. What specific types of flour WILL you allow? Or are ALL types of flour off limits.

➢ CARBOHYDRATES: Many people with a low carbohydrate dietary philosophy succeeded with a rule such as "I will never again eat more than X grams of carbohydrates per Calendar Day." In fact, some people reported successfully using this as their one and only rule.

➤ CALORIES: Similar to carbohydrates, many people had a calorie limit as their one and only rule. For example "I will never again eat more than X calories per Calendar Day." Sometimes this rule had to be revised to a conditional to allow for additional calories after intense exercise *(e.g. "I will never again eat more than X calories + 300 calories/hr. of exercise completed per Calendar Day.)* There were two important "gotchas" which calorie counters ran into. First, especially as they just begin to implement the rule, many calorie counters found their Pigs convinced them to eat most of their calories in junk. Having reached their limit without satisfying their genuine nutritional needs, their bodies would then force them to be less discriminating and they found the limit unsustainable. The other "gotcha" calorie counters often ran into was not having sufficient calories *early enough* in the day. While it would seem to make sense to save calories for later, when the caloric intake becomes too bunched up in any given part of the day it can, for some binge eaters, trigger a binge via the feast and famine response. The solution to this was to add another rule which required a minimum number of calories before a certain time of day. For example, "I will never again eat less than 500 calories before noon on any given Calendar Day."

➤ WHOLE FOODS: Some people succeeded by emphasizing a rule which required them to eat *nothing but* whole foods. "I will only ever eat whole, natural foods again."

➤ ANIMAL PRODUCTS: People who wished to never eat animal products again often phrased their rule in a more emotional way which would consistently remind them of their reason. For example, "I will never again eat anything with a face again" or "I will never eat anything that had a mother."

There's a comprehensive list of possible trigger foods in the free reader bonuses on the website. Just click the big red button and sign up for them.

Please don't mistake the brevity of this "Never Foods" section for a lack of importance. To the contrary, it's often the MOST important section of all. That said, there's much more to learn by looking at how our successful clients defined BEHAVIORS they would never again engage in than foods.

Behaviors

Often, it's a maladaptive behavior more so than a specific trigger food which needs to be eliminated. For example, I've had a lot of clients make major improvements with rules such as "I will never again eat standing up.", "I will never again eat in the car", "I will never eat in front of an electronic screen again", etc. There are also "Always" *behaviors,* but we'll cover them in the next section, along with their suggested translation to Never Rules.

What follows are the more interesting and useful behaviors our clients were using to Cage their Pigs

Eating After Dinner

"I will never again eat after dinner!" Many clients have suggested this one rule nearly completely eliminated their binging since 90% of their binges were at night. The implementation of this rule was supported by several things:

> CUT OFF TIMES: Most clients did not have a specific cut off time because their real lives didn't permit them to eat dinner at the exact same time each day. Instead, they defined "dinner" to end as X number of minutes after they consumed their first calorie of the meal. Generally speaking, the limit was between 45 minutes to 75 minutes, or a little longer if they were at a restaurant. Others suggested dinner was over after they finished one plate of food. Some used both criteria, focusing on whichever took longer. It was important to note our more successful clients did not rush their meals. They wanted to eat mindfully and slowly, so they gave themselves plenty of time to finish, but still with a defined end point. Other people had an absolute time limit for dinner's end which was three hours before bed unless they were out socially.

> EATING START TIMES: When dinner was the end point for daily eating, many clients found it helpful to also create a "start time" for eating the next day, otherwise the Pig might consider a meal in the middle of the night. For example, "I will never again eat after dinner until 6 am on the morning of the next Calendar Day."

➢ BEHAVIORS TO SIGNAL THE END OF DINNER: Many clients had a variety of behavioral signals which made it clear to them dinner was over.

✓ Some people brushed her teeth and rinsed with mouthwash after the meal—they say they don't want to ruin that "fresh feeling."

✓ Some developed the habit of going for a walk after dinner.

✓ Others picked up their crocheting and/or knitting to occupy their hands (especially if they liked to watch TV after dinner).

✓ A few had a hot drink like tea and/or coffee

✓ Some washed the dishes or went to a different part of the house

✓ One woman opened and closed the kitchen cupboard doors, clapped her hands three times in an assertive "dusting off" motion and said "kitchen's closed!"

➢ SIGNIFICANT OTHER SUPPORT: Most successful clients who lived with significant others reported having a heart to heart with their other to request they not offer snacks and/or dessert after dinner. This is not totally required once you've reached a certain level with Never Binge Again because you should be able to control yourself in front of even the biggest pile of Pig Slop by simply telling yourself "That is not my food"... but in the beginning it can be really helpful to create this cocoon around your new habit so it can more easily become ingrained in your being.

Restaurant Rules

Second to Food Rules which governed not eating after dinner, the most frequent behavioral rules used by successful clients were all about eating in restaurants. Many had rules specific to that environment including:

➢ I will never again eat from the breadbasket at a restaurant. This worked particularly well for people who didn't want to give up bread and/or flour as a whole, but had difficulty constrained specifically to the restaurant environment.

➢ I will never again eat out *alone*. People who struggle with sneak eating in particular, and/or those who feared other people's judgment about what they put in their mouth did well with this rule. A variant of was "I will never again eat at a restaurant without being invited by someone else."

➢ I will never again initiate going out to dinner. This rule was utilized by people who'd gotten themselves into food trouble by constantly getting their spouses to take them out.

➢ I will never go to a restaurant again without choosing my meal online beforehand. Most restaurants post their menus online these days. If you make your decisions beforehand, when you're not hungry and/or in the middle of the seductive restaurant environment with all its social pressures, you're likely to make a much better choice. Remember, decisions wear down your willpower, and you don't want to have to rely upon willpower in very tempting situations.

➢ I will never again have hot-milky drinks in a café and/or coffee center.

➢ I will never again attend buffets, weddings, and/or other food-laden events without taking healthy snacks with me (or eat at home first)

➢ I will never eat at a restaurant without checking out it's menu online first – and verify that I have something I'm allowed to it on it

➢ I will never eat at a restaurant more than twice per calendar week (not including work related outings)

➢ I will never order any restaurant dish again without asking for all sauces on the side!

➢ I will never again eat anything from a food court and/or anywhere where plastic plates and cutlery are used.

You don't have to restrict yourself to these rules at a restaurant, the limit is only your imagination. Where do you tend to go overboard, specifically? What do you wish you COULD do in a restaurant if you could only get your Pig out of the way? Then articulate the rule and let the Pig Squeal about it.

Eating While Traveling

The rules clients utilized successfully while traveling seem to have in common a pre-determined, yet very specific loosening of their bullseye. For example **"I will never eat dessert again except for one serving per Calendar Day when I'm away from home for the night."** It's important to note some people *can't* loosen specific rules having to do with sugar, flour, alcohol, and/or other things without getting carried away, but there are usually *some* indulgences they can allow themselves. The point is, the fatigue, new environment, and discombobulation which results from travel can often make us want to throw caution to the wind... but if you think through exactly how you're going to loosen up beforehand, and define the specific limits of that loosening, you needn't strain your willpower.

It's like shooting for the second or third rung of the bullseye on the archery target rather than aiming directly for the bullseye as one does in their everyday life. *(Willpower is fatigued by decision making – so you eliminate the important decisions during your travel by planning limited indulgence up front of one sort or another.)*

Others relied even more steadfastly on key rules which protected them every day. For example, **"I will never eat while driving again"** is a rule even MORE pertinent on longer road trips, and many clients who had this rule clung to it during such events. So is **"I will never again eat anything without having looked up the nutritional information first."**

Some people extended "I will never eat while driving again" to **"I will never eat any food in transit again including trains, planes, automobiles, and/or anything in an airport."** Some limited this to "fast food" only *(anything that comes from a restaurant with a drive through window).*

Still others had rules which ensured they PREPARED for the travel. For example **"I will never again get on an airplane without bringing healthy snacks."** One woman traveled for three consecutive months first used Yelp to find places which might be better for her, then preplanned exactly what to order, and put everything into her food tracker ahead of time. "This makes it harder to change my mind in the moment" she said. She was successful.

Finally, several successful rules pertained specifically to hotel behavior. For example:

> ➤ I will never order room service in a hotel again.

> ➤ I will never again stay at a hotel without asking the manager to empty out the mini-bar before I check in.

> ➤ I will never again eat at a buffet in a hotel.

Eating at Social Events

Often the very specific loosening of Food Rules for social events is done in much the same way aiming at the second or third rung of the archery target is accomplished while traveling. Think through how, specifically, you might like to loosen up and articulate the limits of this indulgence in detail. For example, one successful Never Binge Again person had a rule which said **"I will never again eat more than one meal off of my Food Plan again, and I will only ever eat off-plan again if I'm out with family or friends."**

But more relevant to social events were successful rules which ensured people would NOT arrive hungry, would be prepared, or could compensate for the anticipated indulgence beforehand. For example:

> ➤ **DON'T ARRIVE HUNGRY:** "I will never again attend a social engagement involving food without eating at least 300g of vegetables before I arrive."

> ➤ **BE PREPARED:** Keep an acceptable salad dressing in wallet

and/or purse and ask for salad with the dressing on the side. Bring a healthy version of what's being served, or vegetables which you know won't be cooked in a way you prefer not to consume. *(This way you have things to chew on if you're uncomfortable with the choices wherever you may be.)* Carry beans and/or nuts in my purse. Here's another interesting strategy *"If I'm going to a family gathering, I bring a big plate of veggies to share and/or offer to bring the salad. Then I eat as much greens as I can, and when they ask why I don't want dessert I say something like 'I'm sorry I had way too much food and I'm super full but please, may I have a cup of coffee?'"*

➤ **COMPENSATE BEFOREHAND:** "I tend to eat where I know there are things available for me, and I make allowances in my daily food plan for those meals. For example: whenever my husband has to travel to his rheumatologist, we make a day of it and eat at our favorite BBQ restaurant. The only side they have that comes close to being appropriate for me is fried okra; so, I eat fewer carbs the rest of the day, so I can have about 1/4 cup of the okra at lunch-hubby eats the rest. I get my BBQ sandwich without the bun, and go really light on the sauce" *(Note: Several other successful people fasted during the day if they knew they were going out in the evening in order to compensate for the calories, but I don't endorse that since it can trigger binges by signaling the brain to go into "feast or famine" mode.)*

Some people had a rule which allowed them to compensate afterwards if they were caught in a social situation unprepared. For example **"I will never eat more than one plate of off-plan food at other people's houses again, and I will always skip the next scheduled meal when this happens."**

Successful Never Binge Again people also did their best to avoid going places where they knew there'd be nothing available for them in the first place. For example, one woman received gift certificates for the Lone Star Steakhouse for Christmas, but when she checked their menu online she discovered there'd be no vegetables there she could eat, so she gave the gift certificates to friends. Others avoided buffets entirely.

Finally, one of our Certified Never Binge Again Coaches swears by this rule: **"I will never again eat less than 50% of ANY meal from**

fresh, whole fruits and/or vegetables in every occasion." "Few veggies available means less eating. No fruits or vegetables? No eating!" *(She doesn't let juices, smoothies, or other processed foods count as fruits or vegetables)*

Eating in the Car

I will never again eat in the car! Never eating in the car eliminates most problems with drive throughs and fast food. It also puts a serious dent in sneak eating behavior as the car is one of the primary places people can hide while they binge. This also eliminates grabbing snacks on the way out the door which people generally don't even remember eating. And for those who eat out of boredom on long car rides and/or who binge on junk at truck stops and gas stations on road trips, this rule is a Godsend.

Start Every Meal with Water

I will never eat a meal again without first drinking a full 8 oz glass of water. This reportedly helped people settle their stomachs and feel a little full before they started eating and resulted in better portion control at the meal itself.

Staying hydrated also has a major impact on energy levels and brain function –even mild dehydration in the 1% to 3% range of body weight can often impair brain function. Just a 1.3% fluid loss has also been shown to impair mood in women, and 1.6% is shown to increase anxiety and fatigue in men, as well as diminishing working memory.

References

➤   McKierman, F, Hollis, JH, Mattes, RD (2009). Thirst-drinking, hunger-eating; tight coupling? J Am Diet Assoc. 2009 Mar;109(3):486-90.

➤   Leech, J (2017, June). 7 Science-Based Health Benefits of Drinking Enough Water. [Blog Post]. Retrieved from https://www.healthline.com/nutrition/7-health-benefits-of-water

Going Through the Candy Aisle

"I will never again go through the candy aisle when shopping at the store." After all, if there's nothing but Slop there, what's the point? You don't want to go there, your Pig does.

Many formerly compulsive overeaters report the experience of feeling frozen in front of packaged goods, reading label after label, obsessing about whether or not it's possible for them to buy and/or eat something there. This is a classic symptom of the Pig's hold on our mind. It's perfectly fine that there is this part of our anatomy which wants to eat self-destructive things... but when we allow ourselves to engage in an endless debate about it, we are, in fact, sacrificing our mental wellbeing, as well as our ability to be present and mindful in the world. See how many debates you can END once and for all with Food Rules that make these decisions for you.

Not torturing yourself by staring at things you'll never eat again is a good start.

Note: Some people include the bread aisle in this definition.

Bags, Boxes, and Containers

I will never eat from a bag, box, or container again, except for my own pre-packed and prepared meals. This stops virtually all industrial snacks from squeaking their way into your life, while still permitting the user to do food prep and carry their own meals for safety.

I've always said the goal of the Big Food industry boils down to getting us to look for love at the bottom of a bag, box, or container... and every time you do there's some fat cat in a white suit with a mustache laughing all the way to the bank! Show that guy who's boss with this one simple rule.

Eating from the Refrigerator

I will never again eat directly from the refrigerator. This is a specific instance of the "Food is not food until it's on my plate rule" and forces the user to make a more discrete and specific decision to eat more mindfully.

Eating from the Peanut Butter Jar

"I will never again eat directly from the peanut butter jar" is yet another specific instance intended to raise the user's awareness and necessity to make a specific decision about eating, and be more mindful while they do. Eating directly from the peanut butter jar was a surprisingly common way Never Binge Again users reported getting themselves in trouble with food.

Eating Standing Up

I will never again eat standing up! Eating while standing up and cooking and/or standing at the bar in a restaurant or sports environment is another very common way people reported binging. Eliminating eating while standing forced mindfulness in these locations.

For those who lie in bed and binge, converting this rule to be more specific regarding what position you WILL eat in can be important. For example "I will only ever eat in a sitting down position again." Or sitting at the table with a knife and fork, etc.

Eating on the Couch

I will never again eat while sitting on the couch! This eliminates most of the food binges which occur while watching television. For some people, binging while reading, particularly on salty snacks is eliminated too.

Eating in the Kitchen

I will never again eat in the kitchen. This is frequently paired with "I will only ever eat sitting at a table with a knife, fork, and/ or spoon again."

Eating While Cooking

I will never again eat while I'm cooking.

People who use this rule often have exceptions for making sauces and soups. For example "If I'm making a sauce or soup or something like that I can taste for seasoning but more than twice is eating."

They also note that there is no reason to taste processed foods because they are already finished and cannot be changed, so tasting is eating. These people remind themselves that they're probably about to eat when they're done cooking, and they don't need to eat before they eat just for the sake of eating.

Finally, those who like to bake cookies, cakes, and breads often find it necessary to eliminate the tasting exception completely. They reason that the people they are baking for can tell them what it needs and they can adjust the recipe next time. This requires them to change their reliance on tasting for baking to keeping more detailed track of specific amounts, etc. in their recipes. But for those who love baking but can't eat sugar, flour, etc., this adjustment is well worth it.

Sneak Eating

I will never Sneak Eat again. This is intended for people who have trouble being deceptive about food, feel guilty about it, get overinvolved with this guilt, and use the guilt to fuel subsequent binges once again filled with sneak eating. It's a vicious cycle! But Sneak Eating must be carefully defined in these rules...

One of the most effective definitions we've seen is "I will never again hide food, packaging, and/or any evidence from my partner." Of course, you can substitute "significant other", "children", "spouse", etc. for partner to match your specific situation.

One woman on our free Facebook forum *(www.NeverBingeAgain-Forum.com)* posted a particularly poignant experience which highlights the importance of overcoming Sneak Eating:

> "Recently I was in the middle of the binge when my best friend who lives in the same apartment building as I called and invited himself over. Which is totally fine I love it when he does that. But in my head, I said okay I've got three minutes to hide the evidence. I started running around grabbing wrappers and trying to stash them someplace so he doesn't know. I said to myself This is nuts! This is what alcoholics do! I'm not being judgmental. I used to be an alcoholic. And I used to hide bottles. And this friend is one of my top three biggest supports on the planet! So, I think that if, Heavenly Father forbid, I fall and binge again I'm not going to hide it from him."

Put It On Your Plate First

I will only ever again eat food off my own plate. This stops people from grazing, picking, and overeating on leftovers from others. It creates a distinct eating experience with very clear boundaries. Food is not food unless it is on my plate!

Log It First

I will never again eat anything without logging it first. Some people find logging calories, macros, and nutrition to be extremely tiresome. If that's you, please know it's entirely possible to recover from overeating without doing this. That said, for others the accountability and personal responsibility it provides is huge. They feel their hunger meters have been broken by both their own abuse and the efforts of industrial profiteers, and using an objective, external tool gives them great comfort and control they can't get elsewhere. "I have no idea what amount of food is correct to eat if I don't log it" said one user.

The biggest obstacle confronting food and/or calorie loggers is estimating portion sizes and calorie counts when they're out to dinner and/or at someone else's house. One way around this is to pre-measure about how many ounces of protein/carbs/vegetables are represented by a portion approximately the size of your fist. Then, when you're out you can hold your fist next to the food for a second and estimate with a fair amount of accuracy.

Eating Between Meals

A surprising number of clients reported using the rule "I never eat between meals." It's particularly important to define when a meal specifically begins and ends if you're going to do this, and how much time is required between them. Here's an example you can modify to your needs:

> ➤ A Meal is no more than 60 minutes from the first calorie to the last and/or one plate of food, whichever comes first. Add 30 minutes for a restaurant to allow for serving time. I always allow at least 2 hours from the last calorie of the previous meal to the first calorie of the next one. Some people also add a calorie limit to each meal.

Some additionally allow a snack in addition to the three meals, defined with very specific boundaries too. Usually at least two hours are left between the snack and the meal which both precedes and follows it.

Not eating between meals is particularly good for clients who overdo their food by grazing and nibbling all day long.

Eating While the Pig is Talking

I never eat when the Pig is talking, even if it's just a whisper.

This is actually a Guideline, not a rule, since the presence and/or absence of Pig Squeal can't be externally verified. However, if your Food Rules are worded correctly, then Pig Squeal is defined as any thought, feeling, and/or impulse which suggests you will break them in even the slightest of ways, now or in the future. And since you CAN reliably identify Pig Squeal in your own brain with 100% clarity provided your rules are 100% clear, it's OK to include it.

Never Buy It for Yourself

I will never again buy _____ for myself. I will only ever buy _____ for a guest.

People who implement this rule find it extremely helpful in over-coming sneak eating while still allowing the occasional indul-gence with others.

OK, that marks the end of the successful Never Rule examples for both food and food behaviors. Let's now move on to discuss con-ditionals.

CHAPTER 3:
CONDITIONALS

Deciding on Conditionals vs. Nevers

One of the MOST frequent questions I get from clients is "How do I know if I have to put something in the Never Rules category vs. the Conditional Rules category?" In other words, how do you decide whether you really need to say goodbye to a food *(or food-like substance)* forever, or whether you'll be able to control it in measured quantities and circumstances?

The best procedure is to put off the decision for 30 minutes or so while you engage in a series of mental exercises.

To understand the best answer, you first need to recall the goal of Never Binge Again. We are always looking to maximize TWO outcome variables: Health and Enjoyment...

Successful implementation of NBA means you've maximized your ability to achieve all your health and fitness goals while minimizing restriction of food freedom. In other words, you want to be able to CONFIDENTLY ENJOY YOUR FOOD without interfering with your ability to reach and maintain your ideal body weight, healthy functioning of all bodily systems and organs, any sports performance goals you may have, as well as your sleep, energy levels, and relationships.

It's worth noting this ability also rests on freedom from mental obsession with food—*that torturous internal debate with which we binge eaters are all so familiar*—because without it, there is NO confident enjoyment of anything.

In this context you'll see why my first line of advice is to remind people that, if we were city traffic planners, we wouldn't want to install a stoplight at an intersection which doesn't require it. There are many places in the country, for example, where you can see for miles and miles in all directions. At most, a stop sign provides the necessary safety for the populous. A traffic light would be like slicing a watermelon with a chainsaw...

And often people CAN learn to moderate certain addictive foods with carefully crafted conditional rules. For example, those prone to overindulging on bread in restaurants often report back they've recovered full control when they come up with a rule which clearly constrains a measured indulgence in that environment like "I will never again eat bread in a restaurant except for two slices, but no more than twice per Calendar Week." The reason this works for many is that the decisions are made beforehand, so willpower isn't required at the moment of temptation in the oh-so-seductive restaurant environment.

Therefore, the first step is to carefully assess the safety of "intersection" *(troubled food or food behavior)* as well as what you'd actually be giving up if you let go of it entirely.

How frequently does having even a little lead to a full-blown loss of control? What health risks are involved? What's the worst that could happen if we TRIED a Condition Rule and failed? Make no mistake about it, there IS always a risk. But sometimes that risk really isn't so bad. Only you can know if it's worth taking.

But don't make the decision quite yet. We next need to see what the perceived benefits will be in the Conditional vs. the Never version of the rule. So write out BOTH rules in their full form. For example:

> ➤ I will never again eat bread.

> ➤ I will never again eat bread in a restaurant except for two slices,

but no more than twice per Calendar Week.

Then, ask yourself what would be different in 90 days under the Never scenario. For the purposes of this exercise I suggest you imagine you are going to reassess your rule in 90 days, whichever you chose. So you can think of it as a 90 day experiment. This is NOT really any different than creating a blanket rule since you can always change your Food Plan with forethought and determination, but some people find it's much easier to get the Pig out of the way by calling it an experiment and setting a reminder on their calendar to reassess in 90 days.

Anyway, in 90 days, assuming you followed the Never rule 100% perfectly, what would be different? Weight? Energy? Routines? Emotions? Thinking ability? Skin? Aches and pains? Confidence? Relationships? Work? Home life? Spouse? Kids? Pets? Clothing? Friendships and social activities? Write it out in exquisite detail. Your Pig doesn't want you to see this and will try to get you to rush through it and gloss over what will actually change, so we have to push ourselves to paint a vivid picture.

PLEASE DO THE ABOVE EXERCISE BEFORE YOU READ FURTHER OR YOU WILL RUIN THE EXPERIENCE.

OK, once that's done—and you'll know that it is only when you can emotionally FEEL the future in the most powerful of ways—wipe the slate clean and try again, but this time imagine you complied with the Conditional Rule. Answer the same questions, and push until you can powerfully feel the future.

What we are doing here is assessing your deepest unconscious perceptions and beliefs about how things will play out under each rule. One of three things will happen:

➤ First, you may perceive the Conditional future to be not all that much different than the Never future. If this is the case, you are probably telling yourself you'd like to try the Conditional and attempt to preserve more food freedom.

➤ Second, you may perceive the Conditional future is significantly worse when compared to the Never future you saw before, but still better than where you are right now. If this is the case, you simply need to ask yourself whether it's worth the sacrifice (or speed) of future results as you saw them to attempt the Conditional Rule.

➤ Third, you may perceive the Conditional future to be either exactly the same and/or WORSE than things are right now. If this is the case, it's pretty clear you desire a Never Rule.

Regardless, the decision should be clear at this point.

If you've chosen a Never Rule you may wish to ask yourself if there are any physicians you know who are diagnosing an X deficiency. For example, if you've decided to give up sugar and flour, do you know any doctors diagnosing sugar and flour deficiencies?

Once you HAVE decided, put an END to the debate. Write down your rule along with a reminder to reassess in 90 days. Commit full force to your experiment. You WILL learn something useful that serves you the rest of your days, I promise!

Two last things to share about making Conditional Rule decisions:

➤ COMING TO TERMS WITH NEVER: If you go through more than 3 iterations of unsuccessful attempts to install a Conditional Rule, the odds are you're just trying to avoid accepting that this particular "food" doesn't belong in your life. And your life will be SO much better when you let go of it, despite what your Pig so desperately says. For example, here are the multitude of Conditional Rules for chocolate I tried before finally accepting "I will never eat chocolate again!": (1) "I will never again eat chocolate unless I've done at least two hours of intense aerobics on any given Calendar Day!"; (2) I will never again eat more than 4 oz of chocolate per Calendar Day!; (3) I will never eat chocolate unless it's at least 70% dark; (4) I will never eat chocolate on a weekday again; (5) I will never again eat chocolate alone; (6) I will never again eat chocolate unless I'm at a social event; (7) I will never again eat chocolate without first consuming 8 oz of protein; (8) I will never again eat more than 1 oz of chocolate per Calendar Day; (8) I will never again eat chocolate and pizza on the same Calendar Day; (9) I will never again eat chocolate without first having 16 oz of leafy green vegetables; (10) I will never again eat chocolate unless someone offers it to me; (11) I will never again eat chocolate except for chocolate bunnies; (12) I will never again eat chocolate without first having a kale-banana smoothie; (13) I will never again eat chocolate without hiking a 4,000 foot mountain first that Calendar Day. Eventually, I got the point. I WILL NEVER AGAIN EAT CHOCOLATE. Life is so much better this way! And in retrospect, I didn't have to torture myself. The whole roller coaster incorporated about three years of suffering. I could've been 80% free of cravings in six to eight weeks if I'd been able to let go earlier. Oh well, live and learn!

➢ PROGRESSIVE EXTREMISM: Sometimes people plan a series of conditional rules which gradually desensitize a person to a given food substance they know they need to eventually give up entirely. For example, rather than saying "I will never again eat chocolate", perhaps you first don't eat it before noon each day. Then 4 pm. Then you only eat it on odd numbered days after 4 pm, etc., until you're ready to have none. This has been referred to as "Progressive Extremism" elsewhere. I haven't personally seen people have much success with this approach, but I admittedly don't have a scientific study to prove it one way or the other. I'm presenting it here for consideration for those who wish to experiment.

OK – on to the actual Conditional Rules our successful Never Binge Again implementers reported.

Alcohol

I will never again consume more than two alcoholic drinks per Calendar Day. There seemed to be something about the two-drink limit for women *(three for men)* which persisted across clients. Beyond this they felt their judgment was impaired and it became much harder not to listen to their Pig. At this limit many report successfully sticking to their other rules.

IMPORTANT: Never Binge Again is NOT designed to help people with an alcohol problem stop drinking. Please see Jack Trimpey's work for this if you struggle. You can learn most of what you need to know to quit alcohol for good at www.Rational.org at no charge, though I do recommend you read his books. Mr. Trimpey has been focusing for several decades on the black and white addictions—*those you can quit entirely like alcohol and drugs (as opposed to food where you've got to take the lion out of its cage and walk it around the block a few times each day)*. My system doesn't hold a candle to his when it comes to quitting alcohol and/or drugs. In fact, despite the similarities the casual reader will observe, there are several key differences in Never Binge Again which could actually make an alcohol problem worse if you attempt to use it to quit.

Nuts and Nut Butters

Nuts were a very frequent conditional item. Many people wanted to eat them for the healthy fats they contained, but wanted to limit the overall volume as well as consumption of the salt and oil with which they were often prepared. Accordingly, a variety of successful Conditional Rules popped up

> ➤ I will never eat nuts and/or nut butter again *unless* it's part of a recipe. *(I will never again eat nuts and/or nut butter by itself)*

> ➤ I never eat nuts and/or nut butter *unless* I'm in the presence of others. *(I will never again eat nuts and/or nut butter alone..)*

> ➤ I will never again eat more than one handful of nuts per calendar day.

> ➤ I will never again eat more than two teaspoons of nut butter per calendar day.

> ➤ I will only ever eat peanut butter again with apple slices for breakfast on Saturday and Sunday. *(Very specific meal and day)*

I once recorded a detailed session with a woman who wished to conditionally control nuts. You can listen to it here: https://www.neverbingeagain.com/TheBlog/food-rules/nuts-pausing-and-dessert-control/

Ice Cream

We saw a variety of very creative, successful rules to regulate the consumption of ice cream:

> I will never again eat store bought ice cream and/or eat ice cream at home.

> When buying ice cream outside of a supermarket and/or convenience store environment I will never again eat more than one scoop. *(Combined with the above rule to allow for eating a little ice cream I will never again eat ice cream except for one scoop per Calendar Day within one mile of a beach. (Isolated the behavior to beach days)*

Flour and Sugar

> **HOLIDAY EXCEPTIONS: I will never again eat anything sweet except for whole fruit, berries, and one dessert serving after dinner on Saturdays, Sundays, and Calendar Holidays** (*Christmas, New Years, Valentine's Day, Easter, 4th of July, Halloween, and Thanksgiving*). Many successful Never Binge Again implementers found that allowing just a few Holiday Exceptions gave them just enough leeway to feel "normal" and have something to look forward to, without sacrificing the control they knew they needed to achieve their health and fitness goals.

> **I will never again buy anything with added sugar or grain flour** (*except for 4 or lower on the ingredient list*) **except items for guests which must be eaten within 3 calendar days or thrown away.** Isolating the "buy behavior" was very helpful for many clients, and this particular rule shows how to creatively incorporate exceptions when purchasing for house guests.

> **RESTAURANT EXCEPTIONS: I will never again eat anything sweet except for whole fruit, berries, and one dessert serving in a restaurant no more than twice per Calendar Month.**

Portion Control

> **Never eat directly from a bag or container unless it is snack**

sized. Essentially, avoiding the large bags and containers of processed snack foods help some people tremendously with control.

➤ **I will never again eat anything but a pre-measured portions of any food I've overeaten in the past.** For example, I NEVER eat crisps (UK), nuts, dried fruit, hummus, etc. from a packet or a tub. If you're going to use this one, keep a very specific list of everything you've eaten in the past.

➤ **I will never again eat more than 2/3rds of my plate when eating out and/or at someone's house.** Leaving $1/3^{rd}$ over gives people a better sense of control and reminds them that other third would be for the Pig!

➤ **I will never again finish all the food on my plate.** I will always leave at least one small piece of food on my plate. This is similar to the 2/3rds rule, just a little less allocated to the Pig but it has the same effect.

➤ **When I can't pre-plan a meal, I will never again eat more than one fist sized portion of carbohydrate, one fist sized portion of protein, and two fist sized portions of vegetables.** A portion control device for restaurants.

➤ **I will never again have more than one plate of food at a restaurant.** (Sometimes adding one plate of dessert)

➤ **I will never again go back for seconds at a buffet.**

Pizza

In a large, national survey we commissioned using a stratified random sample of the US population to find out what foods were most addictive, we found pizza topped them all. Almost three times as many people had trouble controlling themselves with pizza vs. chocolate for example. I'm offering this tidbit here to underscore some people may not be able to use ANY pizza rule other than "I will never eat pizza again." If you're having trouble implementing a Conditional Rule about pizza, you may wish to consider that there's no doctor out there diagnosing pizza deficiencies.

That said, the most commonly implemented successful pizza rule was "**I will never again eat more than two slices of pizza at any given meal.**" This is a surprisingly consistent rule reported by dozens of *female* clients. We have NOT run into any men who successfully use Conditional Rules for pizza, I'm not sure why. Perhaps pizza is more addictive to men. Or perhaps men are less willing to restrict it in any form. Regardless, Conditional Pizza Rules seem to be a female thing, at least in our audience.

Food Gifts

I will never again keep Pig Slop received as a gift! I always either give it away or throw it away by the end of the Calendar Day in which it was received.

Eating at Work

I never eat at work and/or accept food from other people "to eat later." The woman who came up with this rule was struggling with treats offered her daily during morning and afternoon teas. She says she never made it until "later" … her Pig always convinced her to eat the extra food quickly.

Time Between Cooked Food Meals

"I will never again wait less than 3 hours from the last bite of a meal containing cooked food until the first bite of the next meal containing cooked food." In other words, this person is able to eat raw food (e.g. fruit and vegetables) between meals if she is hungry but NOT cooked food. This was particularly helpful to her because it encouraged more fruit and vegetables, which were in her unlimited category, and de-emphasized cooked starches, which was where she was getting empty calories.

CHAPTER 4: ALWAYS

These rules were stated in the Always format. You'll see the suggested Never format along side of them. If you skipped the section of the "Six Insights to Make Your Food Plan More Powerful" at the beginning of this book about why Never Rules work better than Always Rules you may wish to read it prior to reviewing the Always Rule examples below.

Water

> **I always drink a glass of water before every meal.** *(I will never begin a meal again without drinking a glass of water first.)* This not only helps people eat less but keeps them more hydrated.

> **Always drink a minimum of 64 ounce of water per calendar day.** *(I will never lay down in bed at night again without having drank 64 ounces of water.)* Similar benefits above

> **I always drink a full glass of water first thing in the morning**. *(I will never again brush my teeth in the morning without first drinking 8 ounces of water.)* Some people combined this rule with the water before every meal rule above.

Vegetables

> **I will always comprise at least HALF of every meal I will ever eat again from vegetables.** *(I will never again eat a meal with less than 50% vegetables.)* This helps assure people they will be satisfied and healthfully nourished.

Weigh and/or Measure

Many people in the deepest grip of compulsive overeating recognize that their hungry and full meters have been *(at least temporarily)* broken. They simply don't know when they're supposed to start and stop eating and can't rely on their intuition and bodily cues. This is currently a very common phenomenon in our society. Remember, Big Food is spending billions to engineer hyperpalatable food-like substances which hit your evolutionary bliss points without giving you enough nutrition to feel satisfied. They are TRYING to overstimulate your hunger meter and break your full meter!

I firmly believe that if we lived in the tropics 100,000 years ago, we could trust our bodies to tell us when to eat and when to stop. Unfortunately, we live in a VERY different environment. There's a fast food joint on almost every corner. There's essentially flavored cardboard used as filler in the food system.

While we are weaning ourselves of excess industrial food, some measure of external portion control is often necessary for some people. Which is not to say that everyone has to weigh and measure their food, but if you're really struggling to comply with your rules, you might not want to dismiss it so quickly. It's less onerous than it seems, and you can make approximations at restaurants and in social situations so it's less obvious to others.

Also, please note that weighing and measuring food does NOT necessarily imply that you also must limit it. It implies you need to KNOW how much you're eating. This gives you the power to adjust later if the weight isn't coming off.

In any case, the form of this Always Rule is very simple: **I will always weigh and/or measure my food before eating it.** *(I will never again consume calories without weighing and measuring them first.)*

Hypothetical Food Plan

The element of surprise is one of the Pig's greatest weapons. It puts you in all sorts of "unplanned for" situations which require you to rely on the very limited resource of willpower to make good decisions. You don't have to go along with this plan!

Instead, force yourself to think through how you might handle any potential trouble spots for the next day by writing out a *hypothetical* food plan before you go to bed. The word hypothetical is critical to the success of this Always Rule. You don't have to 100% stick to the plan you make for the next day, but you DO have to think through anywhere you might get caught unprepared so you can plan for it.

There are also variations on how you might choose to stick to the Plan. For example, perhaps you can't eat exactly what you planned, but you CAN stick to the desired macronutrient balance (carbs/fat/protein) for the meal, or at minimum the calorie content.

Here's the rule: **I will always write a *hypothetical* food plan for the next day before going to bed for the evening.** *(I will never again go to bed for the evening without having written a hypothetical food plan for the next day first.)*

Sue from our Facebook forum (www.NeverBingeAgain-Forum.com) puts the rule another way: "I always plan meals and snacks for the day in advance so I can anticipate any 'wild cards' my day may have in store for me and prepare."

I actually created this rule myself and have used it successfully with dozens of clients. I got the idea for it from a business lecture where I heard Dwight D. Eisenhower quoted:

➤ **"Plans are useless but planning is indispensable."**

➤ **"No battle plan survives contact with the enemy."** Eisenhower was paraphrasing from 19th century Prussian Field Marshall Helmoth Karl Bernhard Grof von Moltke who'd said "The material and moral consequences of every major battle are so far reaching that they usually bring about a completely altered situation, a new basis for the adoption of new measures. One cannot be at all sure that any operational plan will survive the first encounter with the main body of the enemy. Only a lay-man could suppose that the development of a campaign represents the strict application of a prior concept that has been worked out in every detail and followed through to the very end." *(https://bootcampmilitaryfitnessinstitute.com/military-and-outdoor-fitness-articles/no-plan-survives-contact-with-the-enemy/)*

The lecturer went on to explain that businesses with a written business plan AND quarterly/yearly strategy almost never executed the entire strategy as planned. They often diverged greatly from the original plan, sometimes almost completely ignoring it...

BUT...

These businesses were nevertheless MUCH more profitable than businesses who didn't engage in the written planning process! It seems the process of planning forces an essential type of thinking and anticipation, which is most successfully used when the CEO was willing to flexibly veer from the original plan based on contemporary market data.

I asked myself how I might apply this to our battles with the Pig and came up with the hypothetical food plan rule. Many clients tell me it's one of the most useful things I've ever shared.

Smoothies

I always start the day with a healthy smoothie. *(I will never again eat anything on any given Calendar Day before having a healthy smoothie.)* "Healthy smoothie" is then further specified in the Definitions Section of the Food Plan. For example: "A healthy smoothie is at least 16 ounces of water, berries, fruit, and leafy green vegetables." Or however you'd like to define it.

Behaviors

➢ **I will always count to twenty while chewing before swallowing.** *(I will never again swallow a bite of food without counting to twenty while chewing it first.)*

➤ **I will always take a breath between bites.** *(I will never again take a bite of food without breathing first.)*

➤ **I will always eat vegetables with every meal.** *(I never eat a meal without vegetables).* This is a more lenient variation of the "every meal is 50% vegetables" rule.

➤ **I always wait a full hour before eating anything I am craving.** *(I will never again indulge a craving without waiting one full hour.)* Gives time to identify emotional cravings. Most people wind up skipping the indulgence.

➤ **I always eat ONLY 3 meals per day with nothing in between.** *(I will never again eat more than three meals per day, and I never eat between meals).* Some people reduce this to two meals per day. Melissa from our Facebook Forum *(www.NeverBingeAgainForum.com) says* "In terms of losing weight, I thought I needed to force my calories into 3 meals, but each meal was always too small and I was never satisfied after any one meal. When I only eat two meals a day, I am way more successful. I naturally only want 2 meals a day anyway, I've always been like that, so that was an 'aha' moment when I could go back to eating brunch + dinner"

➤ **I always exercise for at least 30 minutes each Calendar Day.** *(I will never again go to bed without having exercised at least 30 minutes on any given Calendar Day.)* I generally recommend a specific number of days each week be added to this rule, as well as an exception for when you have a fever or a doctor tells you to stay in bed.

➤ **I always plan my meals for the week on Sunday.** *(I will never again go to bed on Sunday evening without having planned my meals for the week).* This is a variation on the "write a hypothetical meal plan every night" rule.

➤ **I always cook all my meals for the next day before going to sleep at night.** *(I will never again go to bed on any given Calendar Day without having cooked all my meals for the next day).*

➤ **I will always listen to my Big Why before leaving the house in the morning.** *(I will never again leave the house in the morning on any given Calendar Day without listening to my Big Why).* Note: Your Big Why is the comprehensive list of reasons you want to comply with your Food Plan forever, massaged into a brief essay format.

➤ **I will always make a written accomplishments list before going to bed.** *(I never again go to bed for the evening without having written my accomplishments list for that Calendar Day.)* Stops you from thinking negative and letting the Pig win. A variation on this theme is "I will always state three things that went well which I am grateful for before going to bed on any given Calendar Day." *(I will never again go to bed for the evening on any given Calendar Day without having written at least three things which went well and for which I am grateful)*

➤ **I will always suspend ALL my rules one Calendar Day per Calendar Month.** *(I will never again go a full Calendar Month without suspending ALL my rules for One Calendar Day.)* Although I strongly recommend against this rule for most clients, there ARE some people for whom a planned "off" day allows them to get back to plan the next day, whereas without this rule they put off getting back on track until the tomorrow that never comes.

CHAPTER 5:
UNRESTRICTED

The Unrestricted Rules category, like the Never Rules category, requires much less space to illustrate, but is also of great importance. Specifying which foods and drinks you may have in unrestricted amounts prevents the Pig from telling you "But we'll starve if we don't eat XYZ Slop!"

Please also remember we are NOT recommending you allow ALL of these things in an unrestricted way. For many, some of these items may be trigger foods which belong on the Never list. That said, the full list of things our successful clients allowed themselves in unlimited quantities is included here to stimulate your thinking.

Last, I'm presenting the items used by our successful clients without commenting on their nutritional and/or health value because I don't have the expertise to do so. Use your own judgment please and/or consult with your licensed professional physician, dietitian, etc.

Unrestricted items included non-starchy uncooked and/or steamed vegetables, water, sparkling water, berries, diet soda, black coffee and/or tea with no sugar and/or cream, beans, fresh raw fruit, sugar free gum, leafy greens, lean protein (*mostly grilled chicken and egg whites*) cooked without fat or sugar, no-sugar ketchup, salsa, mustard, apple cider vinegar, lemons, limes, low-calorie broth, stevia, xylitol, vegetable juice, cucumber, and kimchi.

CHAPTER 6:
GUIDELINES

As covered in the beginning of the book, Guidelines are separate from formal Never Binge Again Food Rules because compliance can't be 100% verified and agreed upon by outside observers. Ambiguity is the Pig's best friend, and we don't want to allow ANY in our sacred Food Plans or the Pig will barrel right through. Nevertheless, Guidelines can be very helpful in navigating our day to day decision making with food. Kind of like a good "North Star" to point at.

Successful Guidelines included:

➢ **I always use the present moment to be healthy.**

➢ **I always stop eating the moment I sense I am full.**

➢ **Never feel embarrassed about enforcing rules in front of other people**. It's my body, life, decision. It's their problem if they have opinions about it.

➢ **It is never necessary to finish what's on my plate.**

➢ **I always focus on my success before any failings.**

➢ **I will never dwell on failures.**

➢ **I will always learn from my failures; therefore, they are learning experiences, not failures.**

➢ **I will always follow my rules to perfection – 99% is never enough!**

➢   I always go to bed a little bit hungry.

➢   **Before eating Pig Slop I will always sit quietly and try to feel my toes.** Or take three deep breaths, or count to 100, shut my eyes, breathing exercises, etc. Anything that takes you out of the fight or flight response. Activate the sympathetic system. This is a guideline and not a formal NBA Food Rule because it would defeat the purpose to even suggest to the Pig that you might under any circumstances ever eat Pig Slop.

CHAPTER 7: FINAL WORDS

Please remember, there are some rules with which you won't ever be able to comply. For example, "I will never pee again" is a rule your body will force you to break in a relatively short time. Although it sounds silly, the same is true if you overly restrict your calories or nutrition. Your body will eventually force you to be less discriminating. Food addiction is not just addiction to overeating. Binge eaters are almost always great dieters too. People get addicted to the feast and famine cycle. There's a high associated with both parts.

To recover, you need to step out of the feast and famine cycle and keep a regular course of nutrition and calories flowing through your body. That usually means losing weight slowly – maybe a pound or two per week. "The fastest way to lose weight is slowly", because it's the only way I've seen which doesn't trigger the survival response that causes us to bounce back and gain even more.

For similar reasons, I also counsel clients to use the "soft landing" approach as they're nearing their target weight. Think about it, when send a lander to the moon, we first accelerate the rocket to tens of thousands of miles per hour. But then as we are approaching the moon, we fire the thrusters in the reverse direction to slow down substantially... otherwise we'd crash.

I think it's the same for permanent weight loss. So, when you're within ten pounds of your goal, if you've been losing two pounds per week, I'd suggest you change your Food Plan such that you're only losing one pound per week. Then when you're within five pounds, change it again to lose a half pound. Approach the target weight softly. This way there's no "event" with a sudden switch to throw off the brain and make it think there's a sudden shift in the environment. And we don't have to trigger the survival drive's emergency responses.

Finally, please remember my favorite thing I ever said: "The name of the game is staying in the game until you win the game." People make mistakes no matter how good their Food Rules are. You don't have to let your Pig know that, but on a practical basis, it's true. This is why we want to "commit with perfection and forgive yourself with dignity."

A perfect commitment is the only true commitment possible. "Progress not perfection" as a commitment tool just means you're going to try for a little while until you don't feel like it any-more. Aim with perfection at your bullseye. See the arrow going into the target before you let go of the string. If you miss, analyze the results and do it again. If you hit, do it again. You'll be a better archer before you know it.

Carpe Diem,

Glenn

Made in the USA
Middletown, DE
26 September 2020